AND·THEN·THERE·WAS·ONE

Great auk, extinct c. 1844

AND · THEN THERE · WAS · ONE

The Mysteries of Extinction

BY MARGERY FACKLAM

ILLUSTRATIONS BY PAMELA JOHNSON

SIERRA CLUB BOOKS
San Francisco

LITTLE, BROWN AND COMPANY
Boston • Toronto • London

The Sierra Club, founded in 1892 by John Muir, has devoted itself to the study and protection of the earth's scenic and ecological resources—mountains, wetlands, woodlands, wild shores and rivers, deserts and plains. The publishing program of the Sierra Club offers books to the public as a nonprofit educational service in the hope that they may enlarge the public's understanding of the Club's basic concerns. The Sierra Club has some sixty chapters in the United States and in Canada. For information about how you may participate in its programs to preserve wilderness and the quality of life, please address inquiries to Sierra Club, 730 Polk Street, San Francisco, CA 94109.

A LUCAS • EVANS BOOK

Text copyright © 1990 by Margery Facklam

Illustrations copyright © 1990 by Pamela Johnson

First edition

Library of Congress Cataloging-in-Publication Data

Facklam, Margery.
   And then there was one : the mysteries of extinction / by Margery Facklam ; illustrations by Pamela Johnson.—1st ed.
     p. cm.
   "A Lucas Evans book"—T./p. verso.
   Summary: Examines the many reasons for the extinction and near-extinction of animal species. Discusses how some near-extinctions have been reversed through special breeding programs and legislation to save endangered species.
   1. Extinct animals—Juvenile literature. 2. Endangered species—Juvenile literature. 3. Rare animals—Juvenile literature. 4. Wildlife conservation—Juvenile literature. [1. Extinct animals. 2. Rare animals. 3. Wildlife conservation.] I. Johnson, Pamela, ill. II. Title.
QL88.F33 1990 591.52′9—dc20   89-70133   CIP   AC

Sierra Club Books/Little, Brown children's books

are published by Little, Brown and Company (Inc.) in association with Sierra Club Books.

10 9 8 7 6 5 4 3 2 1

BP

Published simultaneously in Canada by Little, Brown & Company (Canada) Limited

Printed in the United States of America

CONTENTS

1
LONESOME GEORGE

Tortoise hatchling

Lonesome George chomps the fresh leaves brought to him each morning by his keeper. Now and then he stops to look around his yard at the Darwin Research Station on one of the Galápagos (ga-LOP-a-gos) Islands. These thirteen islands are the leftovers of ancient volcanoes in the Pacific Ocean, 600 miles off the coast of South America, right on the equator. George is a tortoise as big as a boulder and almost as still. He's one of a kind: there are no more tortoises exactly like him. George is also a worldwide symbol, a reminder of good news and bad news for animals. The bad news is how we humans have hurried many animals toward extinction. The good news is how much is being done now to try to save the rest.

There are different kinds, or *races,* of tortoise on eight of the Galápagos Islands. Each island has its own kind of tortoise, and each kind of tortoise has a shape and size perfectly suited to life on its own island. George, for example, is a saddle-back tortoise from Pinta Island. His high, arched shell makes it easy for him to stretch his long neck and reach into shrubs for leaves to eat. Once there were thousands of tortoises like George, but in 1971, when scientists searched Pinta Island, George was the only tortoise to be found. The scientists even offered a $10,000 reward to anyone who could find a female tortoise of George's race. But after years of looking, none—neither male nor female—has been discovered.

For centuries, hundreds of thousands of enormous tortoises lived on the Galápagos Islands safe from harm. They had no enemies. Not much can hurt a turtle living in a thick shell as big as a dog house. Nobody even knew about the islands until 1535, when the crew of a Spanish ship found them by accident. The ship was sailing from Panama to Peru when it was carried 500 miles off course by an ocean current, and the sailors found safe harbor among these unknown islands. The Bishop of Panama was a passenger, and when he wrote about the adventure in his native language of Spanish, he described the *galápagos* (tortoises) he had seen. The name stuck; even though Ecuador claimed the islands and officially called them the Columbus Islands, they continued to be known by the name of the tortoises.

In the early days of sailing, no ship could carry enough fresh water and food

Galápagos land tortoise

for the long voyage across the Pacific Ocean. There were no refrigerators or freezers, so sailors had to eat dried and salted foods, unless they were lucky enough to catch fish or find food where they went ashore.

The first sailors to use the Galápagos were pirates, who stored their treasures and supplies in caves along the coasts. After they filled their water barrels from freshwater ponds, they went looking for food. Imagine their joy when they found four-hundred-pound tortoises, lumbering along or wallowing in mud puddles. Here was an endless supply of fresh meat that didn't even have to be chased. It didn't even have to be killed! All they had to do was lug the big reptiles aboard their ships, flip them over on their backs, and stack them one on top of the other. Tortoises can live through long dry spells without food or water because their bodies store large amounts of water and fat. So, sad to say, the tortoises could stay alive for a year in a ship's hold. When the cook

wanted fresh meat, he had only to haul out one of the tortoises and slaughter it.

It wasn't long before every ship crossing the southern Pacific Ocean began using the Galápagos as a rest stop. For the next hundred years, British and American whaling ships captured thousands of tortoises. The logbooks of only a few whaling ships of the United States' fleet in the Pacific during the 1800s show that 96 vessels took more than 13,000 tortoises in 37 years.

To make matters worse, the ships brought an enemy that would continue to threaten tortoises to this day. Black rats scurried off the ships and swam to land or were carried ashore hidden in ships' supplies. It didn't take the rats long to find and feast on tortoise eggs and young.

And then another blow fell. A small colony of people settled on one of the islands. They brought with them cats, dogs, donkeys, goats, pigs, and cattle. The cats, dogs, and pigs ate tortoise eggs and tender young tortoises, which are not

Norway rats eating tortoise eggs

much bigger than a baby's fist. As the donkeys, goats, and cattle were turned loose to graze, they ate plants the tortoises needed, and their hooves trampled tortoise nests. The settlers themselves killed tortoises for meat and oil.

By the 1900s, scientists could see that several of the races of tortoise would soon become extinct. But nothing much was done about it until 1959. Then Ecuador declared the Galápagos Islands a wildlife sanctuary and national park. Many na-

tions and conservation groups now support the Charles Darwin Research Station on the island of Santa Cruz, where Lonesome George lives among tortoises from other islands.

Scientists are determined to keep the other races of tortoise safe. Teams of naturalists and park rangers regularly search the islands for tortoise eggs, which look like hard, smooth tennis balls. When they find a nest, they mark each egg with a number. They take the eggs back to the research station and put them in concrete incubators the size of shoeboxes, where they are warmed by the sun.

When the eggs hatch, anywhere from four to eight months later, a keeper paints a number on the shell of each new baby tortoise—the same number that was on its egg. The number is recorded in a notebook with the baby's weight and measurements. All the tortoises from one island are kept in the same pen, separated from tortoises from other islands, to make sure they don't get mixed up. After a few years, when the tortoises are too big to be eaten by rats, pigs, or other wild animals, they are loaded into boats and taken back to their home islands.

But Lonesome George has not gone back to his island. Scientists are still trying to decide what to do with him. Nobody knows just how long a Galápagos tortoise can live in its native habitat. One lived to be 150 years old in a zoo but might have lived even longer in the wild. Most experts believe that George is middle-aged, perhaps fifty or sixty years old. Some say that George should be allowed to go back to Pinta and live alone. Others think George should just stay in his pleasant yard at the research station, where he gets plenty of food and good care and has the company of his tortoise cousins of other races.

Lonesome George may be the last of his kind, but almost all the other races of giant tortoises are thriving on the Galápagos. They have been saved, but some other animals have not been so lucky.

2
SHAPE UP OR SHIP OUT

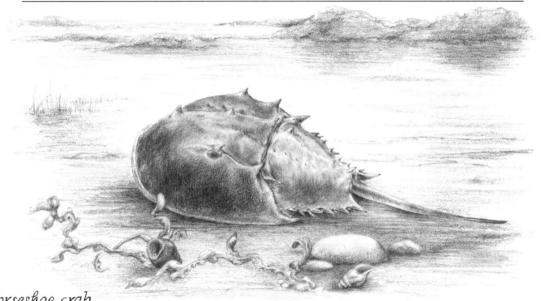

Horseshoe crab

One a day. That was how fast earth's species of plants and animals were disappearing at the end of the 1980s. By the early 1990s, scientists expect, at least one species will vanish every *hour*. By the beginning of the year 2000, there will be one million fewer species of plants and animals on this planet than there were at the beginning of the 1900s. That's pretty scary! What's happening? Is it all our fault?

No species of animal has lived more

than a few million years before becoming extinct (dying out completely) or changing into a different model. Extinction is part of the process of slow change called evolution. From the first moment of life on earth, plants and animals have continually changed and improved, and they will continue to do so. Some are doomed to die off and make way for new species. Some change dramatically. Others change very little from their original design because they are so well suited to their particular niche, or job, in a habitat.

The horseshoe crab is a good ex-ample of an animal that is almost an exact copy of the first models. It's been called a "living fossil" because it's so similar to the ones found in rocks laid down millions of years ago. Horseshoe crabs were, and still are, well adapted to life in muddy ocean bottoms, where they scuttle along in their tanklike armor.

Sharks haven't changed much, either. Three hundred fifty million years ago, long before there were dinosaurs, sharks swam the seas. Judging by fossil shark teeth, we know that prehistoric sharks were much bigger than today's models, but otherwise they're very much alike.

Mackerel shark

Their smaller size is their major adaptation to life as predators in the oceans today.

What does it mean when we say an animal *adapts* to the environment? An adaptation is the development of some trait or feature that increases an animal's fitness for life. But the animal can't just choose an adaptation because it needs it.

If horse breeders want faster racehorses with long, strong legs, they choose and mate the fastest horses with the longest, strongest legs, hoping their offspring will have those same traits. If farmers want to raise dairy cattle with short horns, they do not breed long-horned cattle known for their meat. Instead, they select cattle with the features they know will result in the kind of animal they want.

Nature's way of selecting is a much slower process, and it works by chance. Left to nature, selection is a life-or-death decision. The animal that fits into its habitat best is the one that lives to breed and raise more animals of the same kind. Animals that cannot adapt eventually become extinct. The motto for adaptation might well be, Shape up or ship out.

The horse is a good example of the long, slow process of adaptation. About 60 million years ago, the ancestor of the horse was no bigger than a dog. Fossils of this ancient horse show that it had four toes on its front feet and three toes on its hind feet. From its teeth, we know that it fed on forest underbrush.

But climates changed and lands shifted over millions of years, and the horse changed, too. Several different species of ancient horses became extinct after a few million years because their adaptations didn't work as well as those of some others. Gradually, the horses that survived were the ones with longer and stronger leg bones and with toes fused into a single toenail we call a hoof. These changes made horses better suited to life on the grasslands that had taken over the forests. Tall, fast horses that could see over the long grasses lived longer because they could see predators and out-run them.

Compared to the horse, the peppered moths of Great Britain are quick-change artists. With their light-colored, black-and-white speckled wings, the peppered moths blended into the tree bark. Birds couldn't find them easily. But once in a while, a *mutation* (mew-TAY-shun) would take place. A mutation is a chance of nature that causes an animal to be born slightly different from others of its kind. An all-white animal, called an *albino,* is an example of a mutation. Its opposite, an all-black animal, is called *melanistic* (melon-IS-tic). Whenever a melanistic peppered moth appeared, it stood out against lighter-colored tree bark, and it would be gobbled up by a bird very quickly. Before there were factories, in the 1800s, 90 percent of the peppered moths were light-colored, and only about 10 percent were dark.

But when the new factories began burning soft coal, the air was heavily pol-luted with coal dust and soot. Then the dark-colored moths born by chance were the ones well hidden on the soot-blackened tree bark, and the light-colored moths were easier for the birds to eat. By 1900, 90 percent of the peppered moths were dark, and only 10 percent were light. It was "natural selection" at work. The dark-colored moths lived long enough to lay eggs and produce more dark-colored moths. Many light-colored moths were eaten before they could lay eggs.

Now Great Britain factories have changed from soft coal to cleaner fuel. With less soot blackening the trees, more light-colored moths, born by chance, live long enough to lay eggs that hatch into light-colored moths. Once again, the peppered moth population is adapting to a changed habitat.

An adaptation can be a physical change, such as the longer legs of the horse or the coloring of the moth. But it can also be a change in the way an animal

Peppered moths

raises its young or in what it eats or how it hides. The kind of nest a bird makes, or how many eggs it lays, may be an adaptation to life in a particular kind of forest, meadow, or rocky cliff.

Cockroaches are champion survivors. They crawled the earth long before dinosaurs. Their slim, hard bodies allow them to hide in the tiniest crevices. They eat almost anything, from rotting garbage to the glue in book covers. Their eggs are protected from enemies in a hard capsule, which the mother cockroach hides or carries with her. Their body shape, their ability to eat anything, and the way they protect their young are all adaptations for survival that have worked well for millions of years.

But even an animal that has survived a long time because its adaptations worked can suddenly become extinct. A species can be wiped out in hours or minutes in a disaster that destroys its habitat. When that happens, life starts from scratch.

Part of the nation of Indonesia is the small island of Krakatau, in the Indian Ocean. It is one of three volcanic islands, covered by thick rain forests and teeming with thousands of different plant and animal species. In the summer of 1883, Krakatau exploded. Boiling lava poured from its volcano, down the hillsides and into the sea. Enormous tidal waves wiped out villages, drowning people and animals. The volcano erupted with the force of hundreds of atomic bombs, and all three islands were buried under 200 feet of soot and ashes.

Scientists say the islands were "sterilized." Nothing survived. Nine months later, when the ash was still hot, an expedition of French scientists searched for signs of life on Krakatau. They found one spider. Now, a little more than 100 years later, plants and animals are back, but they're not the same species that were once found there.

The first new life to appear on Krakatau was blue-green algae. Then, as the spores of ferns and the seeds of grasses were carried on winds or in bird droppings, ferns and grasses began to sprout. Just four years after the disaster, the first small trees were seen, and by 1930, the island once again had forests.

Birds and flying insects were the first new animals to appear on Krakatau. Then, in 1888, someone saw one of Indonesia's big monitor lizards that had probably been caught in an ocean current and swept to the island. Soon spiders, aphids, worms, geckos, and other small creatures washed up on the beaches on driftwood and floating vegetation. Animal life on Krakatau and the other islands is not exactly what it was, but scientists are watching closely to see which of these species have the adaptations necessary to thrive in their new environment. An event like the eruption of Krakatau gives scientists a chance to study how species will change as they either adapt to their new environment or die out.

Gecko

3
DEATH OF
THE DINOSAURS

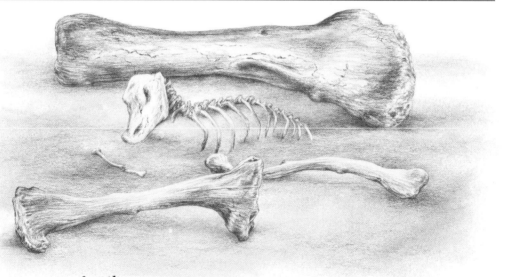

Dinosaur fossils

Dinosaurs dominated the earth for 160 million years—far longer than we humans have. Then, 65 million years ago, they disappeared. Why?

Were the dinosaurs too stupid? Too big? Were their young or eggs eaten by small mammals? Were dinosaurs wiped out by volcanoes? Did the climate get too cold or too hot? Was there a long drought, or did the land get too wet? Did new plants evolve that poisoned the dinosaurs? Did great epidemics of disease spread through them? Nobody knows for sure.

But scientists love a mystery. Because no one ever saw any dinosaurs, scientists have to look for the kind of evidence that police would call "circumstantial." What were the circumstances on this planet when the dinosaurs became extinct? Part of the evidence is found in dinosaur footprints, bones, and other fossil clues.

No one knows how bright or stupid dinosaurs may have been. After all, how do you judge an animal's intelligence? The skulls of some dinosaurs show they had small brains. Others, such as the tyrannosaurs, had big brains, but that didn't seem to matter. None of them survived.

It's likely that small mammals ate dinosaur eggs, but there were just too many dinosaurs of all shapes and sizes for mammals to have eaten enough eggs to kill them all. We know of at least one kind of dinosaur, *Maiasaura* (my-uh-SORE-uh), the "good mother lizard," that traveled in herds of 10,000 or more. The females laid their eggs in colonies of carefully spaced nests, similar to present-day nesting sites of penguins in Antarctica. After the eggs hatched, the female maiasaurs guarded and fed their young until they were big enough to follow the herd. Surely these big dinosaurs could have tromped on or scared away small mammals searching for their eggs. Yet, the maiasaurs died out, too.

John Horner, the scientist who discovered the "good mother lizard," also found one enormous deposit of bones where a huge herd of maiasaurs had been killed by gas and dust from erupting volcanoes. But hundreds of different kinds of dinosaurs were spread so far and wide that it's not likely that a few volcanic eruptions or earthquakes could have destroyed them all.

Dinosaurs didn't disappear in a weekend. Long before the final extinc-

Maiasaur, extinct 65-75 million years ago

tion, there were many dramatic events in nature, such as volcanoes and earthquakes, that wiped out some species. Disease epidemics also proved to be disastrous for many of the dinosaurs that moved out of old territories in search of more plentiful food and new breeding grounds.

As ancient continents began to shift and break apart, new continents were formed. Land bridges across shallow seas appeared where none had been before. Huge herds of Asian dinosaurs paraded across these land bridges in great migrations. That's when they may have met the germs and bacteria that Dr. Robert Bakker calls the "death-dealing tourists."

When Europeans came to the Americas, they brought with them some "death-dealing tourists" such as chicken pox, measles, and other diseases the Native Americans had never had. Many native people died from these diseases because they weren't immune to them; they had no natural protection. It's likely that dinosaurs had no natural protection from the germs they picked up as they moved into new territories. Many dinosaurs could have died, and others, weakened by disease, probably didn't breed or lay eggs or have young.

During the millions of years the dinosaurs lived, the planet was constantly changing. As climates and sea levels shifted, new species of plants and animals appeared as others died out. The dinosaurs had to adapt to these new food supplies and living conditions or die out, too. But one scientist says, "Mass extinctions change the rules." When whole groups of animals disappear, it doesn't seem to matter how strong or fit or well adapted for their habitat they were. In a mass extinction, it's survival of the lucky. The dinosaurs' luck ran out.

Disease, changing food supplies, and growing competition from other animals killed off many species of dinosaurs, but the final blow to the Age of Reptiles may have come from space. Some scientists think that an asteroid or huge meteorite may have crashed into the earth. It would have exploded with a force thousands of times more powerful than that of all the nuclear weapons on earth. Poisonous gases would have swirled around the world in windstorms traveling thousands of miles an hour. The dust and fires would have blackened the skies for months or years. Without sunlight, plants would have died first, and the plant eaters soon after.

Evidence for the asteroid collision idea came from a layer of red clay in Italy that was discovered to contain an element called *iridium* (ear-ID-e-um). Iridium is rare on the earth's surface, but it's common in objects from space. When rock samples from this layer of red clay were tested, they contained thirty times more iridium than had ever been found on earth. When they searched further, scientists found iridium in similar layers of rock around the world. They believe that the iridium came from dust that settled after an asteroid crash. As further

proof for the collision theory, these scientists point out that no dinosaur fossils are found in rock laid down after the iridium dust.

That suggestion set off arguments everywhere. About the only thing scientists agreed on was the fact that mass extinctions have taken place about every 26 million years. But what would make an asteroid arrive on a schedule? So the research went on. Maybe it wasn't an asteroid, they said, but a comet. Comets are "dirty snowballs" from space, and they could have left the iridium clue. There is a great sea of comets called the Oort Cloud surrounding our solar system. But what would make a comet veer off into the earth's path every 26 million years?

Most stars come in pairs, one bright, the other smaller and less brilliant. What if our sun had a small companion star, one whose orbit could take it through the Oort Cloud and cause a scattering of comets? Astronomers are searching for such a distant companion star now. They

Comet

call it Nemesis, the "death star." Other astronomers are looking for Planet X, a tenth planet far beyond Pluto. It would be so far away that its orbit would be able to loop through the Oort Cloud and loosen a shower of comets every 26 million years.

We are halfway through a 26-million-year cycle now, with 13 million years until the next mass extinction. But at the rate we're wiping out wildlife, we may not have to wait for a crash from space. The next great extinction may have already begun.

4
THE HUNTERS

Passenger pigeon, extinct 1914

Martha died on September 1, 1914, in the Cincinnati Zoo. She was the last passenger pigeon on earth. Less than a hundred years earlier, there were so many passenger pigeons in North America that a single flock could block out the sun for eight hours as it flew over a town.

Hundreds of thousands of passenger pigeons roosted and traveled together. In a single flock three miles wide, pigeons flew in layers of twenty or thirty birds. Native Americans and early settlers used passenger pigeons for food because they were tasty and easy to catch. One settler's diary tells how his family used poles to knock 4,000 pigeons from the trees in one day. They plucked the feathers to use for pillows and bedding and threw away the carcasses!

People hated to see the big flocks of pigeons swoop into town, because the birds ate grain and fruit and ruined what was left with their droppings. Millions of pigeons were trapped in nets at their nesting sites and shipped to cities for food. Sometimes trappers lured the birds to the ground with alcohol-soaked grain as bait; other times, they set sulfur fires under trees, where the fumes would cause the birds to drop off the branches.

Trapshooting became a popular sport in the 1800s. A live pigeon was placed in a trap and released with such force that the bird was thrown high into the air so a hunter could shoot it. Today trapshooters targets are hard ceramic disks called "clay pigeons."

In 1857, when the people of Ohio asked for a law that would make it illegal to kill pigeons, one politician said, "The passenger pigeon needs no protection. . . . no ordinary destruction can lessen them." Who could have imagined that hunting would cause the extinction of such an "endless" supply of birds? But it did.

Bison must have seemed to be in endless supply, too. After the Civil War, a news reporter described hundreds of thousands of bison thundering across the prairie. "For forty hours in succession we never lost sight of them," he wrote. At one time, more than 60 million bison roamed the prairies. The "buffalo paths" stamped by bison for centuries became the trails settlers traveled as they moved west.

When crews started to build the Union Pacific Railroad in 1865, profes-

American bison

sional hunters were hired to kill thousands of bison to supply the construction workers with fresh meat. William F. Cody earned the name "Buffalo Bill" when he bragged about killing 4,280 bison in eighteen months.

As pioneer settlements grew, Native Americans fought to keep their hunting grounds. In one of the most shameful events in U.S. history, the government decided to force Native Americans to move by destroying their biggest food supply. Trainloads of hunters were encouraged to head west for the "sport" of killing bison. When a herd of bison galloped by the railroad in clouds of dust, the train slowed, and passengers shot from the open windows until they ran out of bullets. Often they didn't even stop to pick up the carcasses. Some hunting parties would cut out the bison tongues for food, or perhaps take a skin as a trophy. But most animals were left to rot.

In less than twenty years, the bison were close to extinction. By 1889, one small herd of 200 bison lived within the protection of Yellowstone National Park, and perhaps 600 others roamed the plains.

Bison were saved from extinction only because a group of men who cared about them met in the lions' house at the New York Zoological Gardens one December night in 1905. They started the American Bison Association, which saw to it that laws were passed to protect the bison.

We tend to think that humans didn't kill off great numbers of animals before guns were invented, but they did. Not a single weapon was needed to wipe out thousands of Galápagos tortoises. And simple spears brought down the mammoths.

When the first people arrived in North America across the land bridge from Asia, the Great Plains were teeming with huge, shaggy mammoths. Like the animals on the Galápagos Islands, the mammoths had never seen humans before, so they probably didn't run away when hunters surrounded them. Scientists think that tribes killed a mammoth whenever they needed food. Why go to all the work of drying a couple of tons of meat when all you have to do is kill another mammoth? Although they used mammoth skins for clothing and bones for tools, the hunters let most of the dead animal go to waste. How could they have guessed that the mammoths wouldn't last forever?

Like their elephant cousins, mammoths didn't reproduce very quickly, which meant that the mammoth population didn't grow fast enough to replace the ones that were killed. If, for example, twenty calves were born to a herd each year, but forty or fifty grown animals were killed in a year, it didn't take long to wipe out an entire group of animals.

The same thing happened to the moas of New Zealand. Moas were huge, flightless birds that looked like oversized ostriches. The Maori people, who settled New Zealand a thousand years ago, found the moas easy to kill and good to eat. Within 200 years, moas were extinct.

People say "dead as a dodo" when they mean something is done for. The big, flightless dodo birds were found on the Maritius Islands in the Indian Ocean early in the 1600s. When the first dead dodo was taken to a museum, it was thought to be a joke, because no one had ever seen such an odd bird. It was as big as a turkey, with an enormous hooked beak and short, stubby wings. Like a fat, clumsy duck, the dodo couldn't waddle very fast, and it couldn't fly away. Sailors who stopped at the Maritius Islands found it all too easy to club the dodos whenever they needed food. Within 70 years, the dodos were extinct.

The great auk was another flightless bird that vanished fast. It looked like a big penguin with a long, bent beak. Half an hour after the explorer Jacques Cartier landed on an auk breeding ground off Newfoundland, in 1534, his crew had

Dodo, extinct c. 1680

killed enough auks to fill two of the long-boats they used to row ashore. The birds didn't last many years after that, because other sailing ships stopped to collect fresh auk meat, too.

One of the fastest extinctions on record is that of the Stellar's sea cow, a cousin of the manatee that is facing extinction in Florida now. Russian explorers found the thirty-foot-long sea mammal in the Bering Sea in 1741. Twenty-seven years later, they had all been killed.

And so it goes. An animal is found to be useful, and it's treated as just another natural resource, like coal or oil. There's always the feeling that there are more where this came from.

Beavers were trapped as though they'd last forever. Like the beautiful Carolina parakeets that became extinct because their feathers looked pretty on women's hats, beavers almost became extinct because of a fashion in men's hats. Beavers were called "soft gold" because great fortunes were made by companies that paid high prices for beaver pelts. The furs were matted into a fabric called felt and made into top hats for men. By 1700, so many pelts were taken to Montreal that the shippers burned three-quarters of them, because they could charge more money if the furs weren't so easy to get. By 1800, not more than 300 beavers were left in New York State, and the beaver trappers moved west. Beavers were saved from extinction by a change in fashion. When the Prince of Wales began to wear a high silk hat, no one wanted to be seen in an old "beaver."

In the days of wooden sailing ships in the mid-1800s, whalers might kill a hundred whales on a three-year voyage. By the 1930s, "catcher" boats supplied factory ships with 30,000 whales a year, which gave them two and a half million barrels of oil. By the 1960s, they had run

Beaver

out of the biggest whales. With the enormous blue whales and fin whales almost extinct, the industry is going after the smaller sperm whales and minkes. But now they must kill twice as many of the smaller whales in order to get only half as much oil as they once took from the blubber of the larger whales.

In 1980, there were 1,300,000 elephants in Africa. Just ten years later, there are half that number. Elephants are killed for their ivory tusks. In the 1920s, thousands of elephants were killed just to supply Americans with 60,000 ivory billiard balls a year and hundreds of thousands of piano keys. Today most of the ivory goes to Japan and other Far Eastern countries, where it is carved and sold as jewelry, figurines, dice, chopsticks, gun handles, and dozens of other luxuries. Between 1979 and 1987, almost four thousand tons of ivory were shipped to Hong Kong alone. To get that much ivory, more than 400,000 elephants were killed.

Laws have been passed in some African nations to protect the elephants, but that doesn't stop illegal hunters called poachers. Some poachers are native villagers who stalk an elephant on foot and sell a pair of tusks now and then. But most poachers are gangs of men armed with automatic assault rifles that can spray thirty rounds of ammunition a second into a herd of elephants, killing entire families—bulls, cows, and calves. Then the tusks are smuggled out of Africa to countries willing to buy the illegal ivory.

The elephants are not yet extinct, but they are certainly in danger of disappearing. Will we rescue them in the nick of time as we did the bison, or will they go the way of the passenger pigeon?

5
THE IMMIGRANTS

European starlings

Sometimes we don't have to kill animals to drive them to extinction. Sometimes all we have to do is move them around. Humans have been called "the supreme meddlers" because we are never quite satisfied with the world as we find it. Perhaps it's true. People are forever moving animals around, sure they know just the right place for them.

Moving starlings proved to be a big mistake. Europe is the native territory of starlings, but as immigrants to North America, starlings have become major pests as they roost in cities by the thousands or destroy crops in rural areas.

Many new Americans in the late 1800s longed to have European songbirds to remind them of home. In 1890, one recent immigrant ordered sixty pairs of starlings from Europe and released them in New York City's Central Park. Within six years, starlings had spread to Long Island and were well on their way to invading all of North America.

No one suspected that starlings would take over the food and nesting sites of bluebirds, but they did. Bluebirds were once so common in New York State that they were named the state bird. Today, bluebirds are on the endangered species list, close to extinction, while starlings thrive.

As long as a species stays in one habitat, it will adapt to its predators, to the animals that compete for the same food and shelter, and to the parasites and diseases it may pick up in that region. But if an animal is taken from its natural environment and moved to another, it must find new sources of food, hide from different enemies, and fight off different diseases. Sometimes, as with the bluebird, it's the native animals that suffer when the new ones move in.

We humans top the list of animals that cause the extinction of other animals as we move into new environments and take over animals' territories. But second place certainly goes to the rat.

Aboard ships, rats have crossed oceans and landed on every continent man has explored. When they settle on islands, rats do the most damage. When rats move in, the native animals have nowhere to go to escape them. On the Galápagos Islands, rats ate the tortoise eggs. On the island of Jamaica, in the Caribbean Sea, rats caused the extinction of a flightless bird called the rail.

Rails are water birds with strong feet and long toes for walking across soggy marshlands, where they build their nests on the ground. Different members of the rail family live everywhere on earth, except in the polar regions. Thirteen species are extinct, and all of the extinct rails lived on islands.

After the Auckland Islands, near New Zealand, were discovered in 1806, they became a stopping place for whaling ships. The first settlers, in 1807, took with them hogs, cattle, sheep, rabbits, and cats. Uninvited rats went along, too. Less than 60 years later, the native rails were extinct.

The same thing happened on Tahiti, where the red-billed rail became extinct. And the last rail was seen in Jamaica in 1938.

The people of Jamaica tried every way they knew to control the rats, but nothing worked. Then, in 1972, they imported four male and five female mongooses. The mongoose is a member of the weasel family, famous for its brave fights against cobras in India. But along with snakes, the mongoose eats almost anything that moves. The Jamaicans hoped that the mongooses would control the rats.

But apparently nobody remembered that mongooses are *diurnal* (die-URN-al), which means they are active during the day. Rats are *nocturnal* (knock-TURN-al): they're out and about at night. The mongooses began snacking on birds, land crabs, and iguanas they could find in daylight. People didn't get upset until the mongooses started feasting on farmers' poultry, but by then it was too late. Instead of just a rat problem, Jamaica had a rat-and-mongoose problem. Puerto Rico and Hawaii also imported mongooses, with no better luck. (It is against the law to bring a mongoose into the United States, and even a zoo must have special permission to keep them.)

There is also another kind of immigrant that can change the balance of

Mongoose and land iguana

nature—the tame animal gone wild. Each year after Labor Day, when summer visitors go home, the people who live all year on Cape Cod complain about the number of dogs and cats left behind to fend for themselves. It happens at many summer resorts, and on college campuses, too. Some of the pets are taken in by kind neighbors. But others become wild. Escaped or abandoned animals gone wild are called feral (FAIR-el). Packs of feral dogs roam most of our big cities, and feral cats live everywhere, preying upon birds as well as small mammals such as rats, mice, and gophers.

We've seen what happens when feral pigs, donkeys, goats, and other animals were left behind on the Galápagos and other islands. Not only did they take over the food and territories of native island animals, but they preyed upon them as well. Who knows what might happen to the birds and small mammals in rural areas and suburbs as they compete for food and shelter with the growing numbers of feral cats and dogs?

6
NO PLACE TO LIVE

Sea otter

When the oil tanker *Exxon Valdez* hit a reef in Alaska's Prince William Sound, on March 24, 1989, eleven million gallons of crude oil oozed out. In a few days, miles of the thick, sticky, stubborn, smelly, black oil had coated more than 700 miles of coastline. Two hundred miles from the spill, beaches were so slick that not even snails could cling to the rocks. Oil stuck to the feathers of a quarter of a million water birds. They couldn't fly or stay afloat. Most of them died.

Almost a thousand sea otters died when their fur was plastered with oil. The fur of sea mammals traps air that serves as insulation from the cold. When it is slicked down with oil, the animals can't keep warm in the cold ocean. Even though volunteers cleaned hundreds of otters and returned them to the sea, many otters will still die from eating oil-soaked fish. Will the oil spill cause animals to become extinct? Probably not. But the oceans can't withstand many oil spills without putting all marine life in danger.

More than by hunting or by moving animals to foreign places, we are causing the fastest rate of extinction since the dinosaurs by ruining whole habitats. Oil spills are only one way of polluting water. We also dump hazardous wastes, such as leftovers from nuclear industries and some kinds of chemicals, in the seas, lakes, and rivers.

"Good" garbage is *biodegradable* (bi-o-de-GRADE-u-bul). It will rot. Plastic won't rot. Aluminum cans will last longer than the pyramids of Egypt. Plastic garbage bags may float for centuries in the ocean where they can choke seals and dolphins. The plastic holder from a six-pack of cans tossed aside today might trap an animal twenty years from now.

One of the hardest problems to solve is what to do with radioactive wastes from nuclear medicine and nuclear-powered industries. Such material must be carefully sealed because it keeps giving off harmful rays for many years. When it's dumped in the ocean, there's a danger that, in time, the radioactive waste containers might leak or break open. If that happens, marine animals and plants for miles around will die.

Coral reefs are like supercondos with billions of tiny rooms. Each room is the skeleton of a minute coral animal called a polyp (POL-ip). A coral reef isn't built in a hurry. It takes millions of years

Sea gull trapped by plastic six-pack holder

for a reef to become the size of Australia's Great Barrier Reef, which is bigger than anything ever built by humans.

We get tons of food from the fish, crabs, lobsters, and other animals that live in and around coral reefs. And even though we know that coral reefs protect shorelines from erosion, we are blasting the coral and dredging to make deeper harbors. Or we're covering the reefs over to put up more buildings. We can't get them back, not for millions of years.

When it was first developed, every-one welcomed the pesticide DDT as the best thing ever to happen to agriculture. Here at last was a way to wipe out crop-eating insects. And no more mosquitoes! But no one counted on the other things DDT would do.

When a lot of polar bears were dying in the Arctic, scientists wanted to know why. They were surprised to discover the bears were full of DDT. How could that be? No one had sprayed the Arctic with pesticide.

What we hadn't known was that

Polar bear and cubs

DDT works its way up the food chain. The DDT that reached the polar bears actually came from California fruit orchards. When fruit growers sprayed their trees, DDT was carried by winds out over the ocean. There it settled on algae and seaweed and on the masses of tiny floating animals called plankton, which many fish and whales feed on. When the fish swam north, they were eaten by polar bears. DDT stayed in the fish, but even more stayed in the polar bears. The bigger the animal, the more DDT built up in its system.

Birds suffered, too. Even though DDT did not kill birds directly, it caused them to lay eggs with such thin, brittle shells that the eggs broke in the nests. Brown pelicans were once so common along southern coasts that fishermen had to shoo them away. When pelicans became scarce, scientists visited their nesting grounds. In one colony of 300 nests, they found only 12 whole eggs. All around lay crushed and broken eggshells. When the eggshells were taken to a laboratory and tested, they were found to contain DDT from contaminated fish the birds had eaten.

If a person eats fruit sprayed with DDT, the pesticide does not leave the body for a long time. It was only when human babies began getting sick because their mothers' milk contained DDT that the pesticide was finally outlawed.

Only a few hundred tigers still stalk the jungles of India and Nepal. Many were killed by hunters. But what really killed off the tiger—though not directly, of course—was an insect spray. Strangely enough, mosquitoes *protected* the tigers and many other jungle animals because the insects kept people away. Few people could stay long in a mosquito-infested tropical rain forest, where yellow fever, malaria, or other diseases carried by mosquitoes were bound to infect them. But DDT and other pesticides made it possible to wipe out the mosquitoes and open that land to farmers and tourists.

Rain forest destruction

When their territory is gone, the large animals can't "make a living." No longer is there room for many tigers to hunt in what is left of the jungle.

In a wide belt around the equator, tropical rain forests are swarming with life. Although rain forests take up only a sixth of the earth's surface, they are home to almost half the world's plant and animal species. Scientists believe there are thousands, and maybe millions, of species in the rain forests that haven't even been described and named, or perhaps even found yet. Among these may be plants we could use for medicine or food. What fascinating birds or reptiles or insects are we missing?

We may never know. The tropical rain forests are disappearing at the rate of 50 acres every minute! That's like mowing down the whole state of West Virginia every year. Trees are cut for lumber or bulldozed down to make room for farms and towns. When Dr. Jane Goodall went to Africa to study chimpanzees in Kenya in 1960, the chimpanzees had a territory of sixty square miles. Today the chimps of Kenya are limited to a two-mile strip of forest. The great jungles of Indonesia, home of the orangutans, are being cut down for lumber, and much of the exported wood is used to make throwaway plywood forms to mold concrete for buildings.

It's been said that when America was new, with only thirteen states, the forests were so thick that a squirrel could hop from tree to tree all the way from Maine to Florida and never touch ground. Not so today. Our large forests are few and far between, and even those are now in danger. A major problem is *acid rain*. It sounds like something from a monster movie, but it's not. It's real rain, but it's full of chemicals from factories, and it eats tree bark and leaves. It seeps into the forest floor and poisons the soil. It falls into lakes and ponds and kills the fish. Acid rain is carried around the world on currents of air. Silent and invisible, it kills plants and animals and even eats into stone.

Wetlands are not wastelands. They teem with life, but they're disappearing fast. Bogs, swamps, and marshes are being filled in to make room for waterfront apartments and hotels. The Everglades in Florida is a shallow river of grass that once covered seven million acres. It was alive with millions of water birds and other animals. But now, more than half of it has been drained to make room for farms, industries, and homes. Miami is one of the world's fastest growing cities. One hundred thousand people settle there each year, and ten million tourists visit. Each person uses 200 gallons of water a day, and all of it must come from the Everglades. It's no wonder there is less and less space for alligators, manatees, and water birds.

In the United States alone, we are paving over more than 3 million acres for cities, highways, airports, and water projects *each year*. Where mankind moves in, must animals always move out? Or can we find ways to make room for all creatures?

7
AND NOW
THE GOOD NEWS

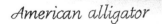
American alligator

A "doomsday" book lists all the animals in danger of extinction. Its official name is *The Red Data Book*. It's published each year by the International Union for Conservation of Nature and Natural Resources. In a book of so much bad news, can we ever find anything good?

The good news is that some animals get off the list, when they make a comeback. The American alligator was once in danger of extinction because a lot of people thought that alligator skin looked better on shoes and luggage than on the alligator. Then a law was passed in the 1970s to protect the big reptiles from harm. Now there are so many alligators that they are causing problems. They are turning up on golf courses and in private lakes. One huge alligator was found basking in the sun on a runway at the West Palm Beach International Airport. The alligator population is up to a million, and some way must be found for alligators and people to live side by side.

When a large predator like the alligator thrives, dozens of smaller animals thrive with it. Alligators make room for an entire community in their water holes. Fish, turtles, snakes, frogs, and snails settle in. Herons, ibis, egrets, spoonbills, and other birds stay close because they can find food, and so do raccoons, muskrats, wild pigs, and other mammals. As long as the alligator keeps the water hole weeded and open, the whole community lives well.

Protecting a large animal is a real bargain because it saves whole ecosystems. When we protect one habitat, we help all the animals that live there. In order to help the African elephant, we must help all the animals of the Serengeti. In that 5,000-square-mile area, there are more than 400 species of birds, 50 kinds of mammals, and tens of thousands of insects and other invertebrates.

Zoos and wildlife sanctuaries are part of the good news. About 90 percent of the mammals and 75 percent of the birds in American zoos were born in captivity. No longer can an expedition go into the jungle and capture a tiger or monkeys. No one is allowed to catch a dolphin in the open ocean for a marine exhibit or research without permission from the government. Unfortunately, many dolphins, seals, and sea turtles are trapped illegally in fishing nets that trail for miles behind commercial fishing ships. People are trying to design safer nets that will allow turtles and sea mammals to escape if they are caught. They are also trying out different regulations that would require fishing ships to haul in nets more frequently, which could save large animals caught in them from drowning.

Zoos were once prisons of concrete cages and iron bars. Although some are still prisons, the best zoos display animals in large areas much like the animals' own habitats. Many rare animals have bred and raised their young in zoos, but it's not always easy. Panda babies are rare enough in nature and rarer still in zoos. Only 1,000 pandas live in their native China and Tibet, and only 100 in zoos around the world. Three zoos outside of China—in Mexico, Madrid, and Tokyo—have raised panda cubs. Ling-Ling, a panda at the National Zoo in Washington, D.C., has given birth to several cubs, but none has lived more than a few hours despite careful veterinary care.

For many wildlife experts, the big goal is to breed animals in captivity and return them to their native homes. But that's not as easy as it sounds. You might think that all you'd have to do is open a cage to let an animal know it's free, but that doesn't always work. In Indonesia, workers at one rehabilitation center try to move once-captive orangutans back into the jungle, but many of the animals won't go. The big red apes like to hang around the feeding station, where bananas and other good food are handed out. When workers take them by the hand and lead them into the forests, some orangutans drag their feet like ornery children. A few may stay alone in the forest overnight, but the next morning they are back in time for breakfast. Part of the problem is too little forest and too many captured orangutans that need homes in it.

The National Wildlife Refuge System cares for 400 habitats from the Florida Keys to Alaska. They protect green sea turtles and monk seals in Hawaii, whoop-

Panda

ing cranes in Texas, and trumpeter swans in Montana. They provide safe feeding and resting grounds for the annual migrations of thousands of ducks, geese, and other birds.

Bald eagles have found help in the refuge system, too. When the eagle was chosen as our national symbol in 1782, there were probably 75,000 of the big birds nesting in the U.S. territory. Today there are fewer than 3,000. It wasn't until 1940, when bald eagles were on the edge

Bald eagle chick

of extinction, that Congress passed a law to protect them. But even when they were safe from hunters, eagles' eggs were destroyed by DDT because the adult birds had eaten fish contaminated by the pesticide.

Now the wildlife experts take the first clutch of eggs from an eagle's nest and put them in an incubator until they hatch. With her eggs gone, the eagle will lay a second clutch of eggs, which she will raise. When an eagle is found without eggs, or whose chicks have died, the scientists place three-week-old eaglets from an incubator in its nest. The foster parents usually adopt the chicks and raise them as their own.

Sometimes they use a process called *hacking*. Rangers build nests on platforms high atop towers in wilderness areas where there are no eagles. They place eight-week-old eaglets in these nests. At first, humans feed the eaglets, although they are careful to stay out of sight. They use a puppet that looks like an eagle, because they don't want the young eagles to *imprint* on humans. The first moving object a newly hatched baby bird sees is "imprinted" on its brain as its mother. Gradually, the eaglets are fed less and less to encourage them to fly off and hunt their own prey. It's a long, slow process, but it works.

The whooping crane is another success story. In 1941, there were only sixteen whooping cranes, but now there are more than 200. They are still on the endangered list, but their numbers are growing.

The Endangered Species Act became law in 1973. It makes it a crime for anyone to sell or transport an endangered species or a product made from the body of an endangered species. That means people can't sell rhinoceros horns or tiger skins. No longer can certain tropical birds be transported or sold or kept as pets. It is illegal for an endangered animal to be "killed, hunted, collected, harassed, harmed, pursued, shot, trapped, wounded, or captured." The law also sets aside some "critical" habitats for some species. That means that no federal government agency can use the habitat of an endangered species. Unfortunately, it does not protect the same area from private projects. For example, where an eagle is nesting, a federal highway or an army base can't be built because it's paid for by our taxes. But someone might be able to build houses or a shopping mall or a factory, unless state or local governments protect the land.

The shy, bashful marine mammal called a manatee is a distant cousin to the elephant, although it looks like a cross between a seal and a baby hippo. Some grow to be 12 feet long and weigh 3,000 pounds. They used to live a quiet life in Florida's waterways, but there are few left. Now they must compete with hundreds of thousands of small power

Manatee

boats. Someone has said that the manatee is going off the earth for the same reason that television shows go off the air—no sponsor. Who will sponsor the gentle manatee and other animals that cannot speak for themselves?

It's easy to get people interested in saving cuddly animals such as pandas and baby seals, or elegant, dramatic animals such as tigers and snow leopards. But what about a butterfly or a tiny fish called the snail darter? Should those be saved? Does it matter that the last dusky sparrow died in 1989?

We tend to forget that we are the only creatures who can make choices. Instead of adapting to an environment, we can change it. If we're cold, we can put on warm clothes and turn up the heat. Too hot? Just turn on the air conditioner. Want to fly? Just get on an airplane. Run out of food? Buy groceries from anywhere on earth at the supermarket. We can change the rules. We are the animals with imagination and power.

All creatures large and small have the right to live because they share their home planet with us. We can do nothing about the way animals adapt to the changes in the environment, but we *can* do something about how the environment changes. We can keep the earth clean. We can stop polluting and destroying the habitats of other living things. We can learn from the past and begin planning for the future.

INDEX